S0-AHO-076

Love and Fruitfulness in the Bible

Love and Fruitfulness in the Bible

by A. M. DUBARLE, O. P.

Translated by Religious Book Consultants

ST. NORBERT ABBEY PRESS
De Pere, Wisconsin
U. S. A.
1968

ST. JOSEPH'S UNIVERSITY   STX

680.S5D813
Love and fruitfulness in the Bible

3 9353 00005 4260

BS
680
S5
D813

110698

Excerpts from *The Jerusalem Bible,* copyright © 1966 by Darton, Longman & Todd, Ltd. and Doubleday and Company, Inc. Used by permission of the publishers.

Edited by Lisa McGaw

Translated by
Religious Book Consultants

Originally published in French under the title *Amour et Fecondite dans La Bible* by Editioni Edouard Privat, Toulouse, France.

© 1968 St. Norbert Abbey Press

Standard Book Number 8316-1028-x
Library of Congress Catalog Card Number 68-58124

Printed in the United States of America
ST. NORBERT ABBEY PRESS
De Pere, Wisconsin 54115

CONTENTS

FOREWORD

The present study developed from a shorter article which previously appeared with the same title in the series "Recherches et débats du C.C.I.F.," No. 43: "Sexualité et limitation des naissances" (June, 1963), pp. 105-121. I am grateful to the publisher, A. Fayard, and to the editors of the series for permission to use this text again. I have been able to enlarge the topic somewhat in reworking it for independent publication. This new edition is about three times as long as the first article, but it has preserved the original content with slight modifications. Although I sought to gather the essence of the biblical teaching on my chosen theme, I have tried to avoid a presentation too technical or difficult, so as not to discourage educated readers who are nevertheless not specialists in theology.

My confreres, the Fathers Régamey and Hubert, aided me in the selection of some illustrations. May I express my gratitude to them here.

INTRODUCTION:

THE WORD OF GOD
AND HUMAN LEARNING

Studies concerning sexuality and marriage are multiplying in our day; attention is focused on this factor of the human condition. Men seek the sense and the rule which will best assure its place in a harmonious life. The Christian, for whom human existence and therefore sexuality cannot be exempt from regulation by faith, looks for light on this subject in inspired Scripture, the richest and most authentic expression of God's Word. It is not out of place here to indicate briefly what he can expect to find.

The biblical authors suppose an elementary knowledge of the data accessible to our common experience. They have no intention of examining in detail all the richness of these data, whether they be astronomical, meteorological, biological, social, political, or geographical. They are ordinarily satisfied with the summary view held by their average contemporary. Their goal is to show the relationship of these natural realities to God and to an upright religious life. Just as we should not expect a highly developed astronomy from the Bible, yet we do find there the profound feeling of adoration which ought to be awakened in our hearts by the sight of a world incommensurable with man (Ps. 8), so we should not expect from the Bible results of an exhaustive inquiry into all the possible forms of marriage and of sexual regulation, although we do find related there the steps of a progressive discovery of the providential meaning of the sexes in a human life conformed to the design of the Creator.

Research concerned with factual knowledge and description has taught us the wide variety of social forms within which sexuality is lived. It has shown that human nature is much more adaptable than we would have thought with an experience restricted to our single cultural milieu or with the limited information the Bible gives about ancient civilization. The Bible does not say everything that can in fact be known about man and the universe. Furthermore, the Word of God heard in the Bible is expressed in terms of determined social structures; sometimes one political or economic system (such as the monarchy or small peasant ownership) seems to be presumed as the ideal or even the only possible system.

These facts have practical consequences for reading the biblical texts. Implicitly or explicitly, the inspired authors refer to a nature. They admit that, even before any revealed divine law, certain rules of conduct are imposed by virtue of a natural structure of man, set up by the Creator, and that these rules are not subject to the simple arbitrariness of human wills. But knowing little beyond their own social milieu and the surrounding pagan world, the inspired authors were led to consider natural whatever was admitted as moral. Today, with our wider knowledge, we should try, in reading the ancient biblical writings, to discern what is natural in the sense of a structure found always and everywhere, and what is natural in the sense of valid in a certain milieu, even independently of the Mosaic law and of the gospel. We must constantly strive not to bind the Word of God to the conditions of life of its first recipients—conditions which are no longer our own; on the other hand, we must be on our guard not to deny any of its relevance for our lives today, which move in a different culture. It is not a question of choosing as we wish from the biblical witness, but of being integrally faithful to it by careful attention to the finest nuances of the texts. For the inspired writers sometimes give subtle indications that they realize they are speaking according to the very views of the creative wisdom or, in other circumstances, according to the respectable but not unchangeable convictions of a given concrete society.

If we take these precautions, study of the Bible will be fruitful. It will not render useless all the positive inquiries that can be conducted in our day. But it will allow theologian and faithful alike to come into contact with the richness of divine revelation at its source and subsequently to arrange what human knowledge has acquired according to revelation's viewpoints.

Therefore our direct concern here will not be facts, customs, or laws concerning the family or the couple in the people of Israel, insofar as this would simply describe ordinary concepts and behavior in a given culture comparable to others of the ancient East.[1] We will allude to these things only when it will help us to understand a teaching that remains always valid for us as Christians, a teaching summed up in the two words "love" and "fruitfulness."

These are, in fact, the two main directives which the Bible sees in the fact of different sexes and the consequent behavior. In the biblical and Christian view, these values are normally realized in marriage. This will be assumed in our study; and we will not deal here with marriage as such, or with the laws regulating entry into and life within this institution. Despite the place they occupy in the Bible, the problems of polygamy or monogamy, of divorce or indissolubility, and the forms of sexual misconduct will not be treated directly. Rather, we will concentrate on the positive content of sexuality and marriage.

From the beginning of the sacred collection, in the two creation accounts found in Genesis (1:1-2:4 and 2:4-25), the two aspects of sexuality mentioned above are expressed. It is most natural to start from there, and to continue with the development and enrichment of this double theme in the following books.

[1]The reader will find such a detailed description in R. de Vaux, **Les institutions de l'Ancien Testament,** Vol. 1 (1958), pp. 37-87.

I

FRUITFULNESS AND THE IMAGE OF GOD

The account of the six days of creation (the first account in the present literary arrangement, though more recent by date of composition) presents an attempt at methodical inventory and classification of created beings. After creating the plants and the various groups of aquatic, aerial, and land animals, God decides to create man in His image, to dominate the earth: "God created man in the image of himself, / in the image of God he created him, / male and female he created them" (Gen. 1:27).

The words used are not "man" and "woman," with their psychological and social implications, but "male" and "female," terms equally applicable to animals. In the encyclopedic view of the narrator, animal sexuality and human sexuality are comparable in terms of a common goal: reproduction. The blessings bestowed on beasts (1:22) and on men (1:28) are identical in the terms: "Be fruitful, multiply, fill the earth (the sea)." This blessing of fruitfulness does not add to sexuality a capacity which would otherwise be foreign to it; it only makes explicit what normally belongs to sexuality. Human language cannot say everything at once; hence we find those parallel and synonymous expressions so dear to Semitic writers for things which are not really multiple. God assigns to each group the appropriate foods: to men the grain and fruit, to animals the green plant. Thus the Creator provides for the continuance of life by giving the faculty of generation and the necessary sustenance. The biological meaning of sex, fruitfulness, is therefore what this account is trying to express in the first place.

Yet secondary meanings can be discovered in this text. Man, created in the image of God, is consequently superior to the animal and is destined to dominate it. In the blessing bestowed on man, this special prerogative is added to the order to multiply, common to animal and to man. This natural superiority should have repercussions on the relationships between individuals of different sexes; we can at least assume this, if not read it expressly in these verses. God creates man in His image; the different individuals, the male and the female, are equally in His image. They will not mate simply like the animals.

Nevertheless, this should not imply that the diversity of the sexes is for Genesis the immediate basis of the divine image in man, as if the inspired author, anticipating the plurality of divine persons taught by the Christian dogma of the Trinity, saw its image in the diversity of sexes within the human species.[1] It is important to insist upon this, to avoid blurring at the outset a fundamental biblical view and idealizing excessively the fact of sexuality.

Israel's religion had to wage a long struggle against pagan polytheism, which admitted not only many gods but divine couples of a god and a goddess. For ancient paganism, sexual fruitfulness was a property common to gods and creatures. Nature cults celebrated and represented in their sensual rites this divine fruitfulness, intending in this way to assure the fruitfulness of human society and of the flocks and fields. The prophets violently condemned the orgiastic aspect of foreign religions. A sacred book could hardly present a doctrine liable to be twisted in a carnal direction and likely to appear to legitimate pagan ideas and practices.

Furthermore, for Israel's thought as for that of her environment, birth is the remedy for death.[2] This is not stated explicitly in the account of the "very good" creation, where only the positive aspect is expressed: "Increase and multiply"; but it can be forgotten only with difficulty. To suggest in God a transcendent prototype of generative sexuality could have led to the thought that there was in Him the possibility of death; the authentic faith of Israel could not permit this.

We find, on the contrary, that the Old Testament is loath to recognize sexual attributes in God; this is probably why it did not present the duality of the sexes as the basis of the image of God. The very vigorous anthropomorphism of the biblical writers stops short of the sexual domain. Even in the conjugal allegories, where the prophets describe the alliance between God and His people as a marriage, they spontaneously avoid all properly sexual imagery, even though they do speak of the children which Yahweh's spouse gives Him. Yet they do not hesitate to use the crudest language to stigmatize Israel's prostitutions with her lovers, the pagan divinities (Ezek. 16:25; 23:2-20).

This clear separation of the sexual and the divine in the choice of anthropomorphic expressions is found again in ritual laws. Sexual activities—whether legiti- mate or not morally, healthy or pathological medically —involve longer or shorter periods of ceremonial im- purity, intended to separate them far from cultic activities in everyday life.[3] This does not proceed from rigorism or from an overdeveloped fear of pagan contagion, but from a religious concern to avoid the degrading confusion of the divine and the sexual so common in the ancient Near East.

If the biblical writers experienced the incompati- bility of the two domains so deeply, it is because Yahweh possessed for them a transcendent perfection which surpassed the divisions and oppositions observ- able in creatures. Very often in the sacred text we find double phrases meaning that the divine being or the divine action is not limited by any of the categories of the creature: Yahweh is God when near and when far away (Jer. 23:23). He is the first and the last (Isa. 41:4). He deals death and life (Deut. 32:39). He forms the light and creates the dark (Isa. 45:7). He has made the rich and the poor (Prov. 22:2). We could multiply the examples. From such a point of view, to attribute a sex to God would be to limit

Him, to forget that He is the All (Sirach 43:27), out-side of whom there is nothing, but who has made His works in pairs (Sirach 33:15).

God made man in His image; man is only a creature, not a God. An essential mark of the finite-ness that belongs to man as creature is the difference of the sexes. The whole account of the six days shows the Creator producing His works by His Word, and distinguishing their parts: in humanity, too, God distributes among distinct subjects capacities diverse and indispensable to one another. No indivdual can be effective by himself; he needs the cooperation of a complementary individual. Even to reproduce, the male and the female must be in union.

God made man in His image. Somewhat as a son is in the image of his father (Gen. 5:1-3), every human being possesses an essential relationship to his Author, who is also his transcendent Model. But man is male and female. Every human being is at least in a virtual relationship with an individual of the opposite sex, without whose cooperation he cannot perpetuate himself. In singling out sexual difference as the notable characteristic above all the other internal differences realized in humanity, the sacred author indicates the importance he attaches to it. In naming it next to the image of God in the descriptive defin-ition that he gives of man, the narrator lets it be understood that at least in the human species, it is not simply a biological function. But he says no more than this.

Later St. Paul, meditating on this text of Genesis, will find support for some profound insights. Man the sinner, who in his pride refuses to honor or to thank God as He deserves, falls blind and fails to recognize that he is made in the image of God. Reversing the order, he makes gods for himself in his own image, gods with the same weaknesses and limits as man himself (Rom. 1:21-23). Paul anticipates the frivolous sarcasm of Voltaire, but with tragic seriousness: "Si Dieu nous a faits à son image, nous le lui avons bien rendu."[4] When the creature fails to recognize or corrupts his relationship to the God whose image he is, he comes fatally to do the same to the relationship between the sexes. "Their women have turned from natural intercourse to unnatural practices, and their menfolk have given up natural intercourse to be consumed with passion for each other, men doing shameless things with men and getting an appropriate reward for their perversion" (Rom. 1:26-27). By attracting attention to the degradation of what is deepest and most basic in the divinely established order (Gen. 1:27), Paul has pointed out that man's sexuality is much more than a mechanism intended to assure the continuance of the species. It touches essential roots of our creaturely condition and of our attitudes toward another. This is what the account of the creation of woman in Eden will make explicit.

Before considering this account, we must look at another passage where St. Paul was again inspired by the text of Genesis on the image of God in man. His commentary is paradoxical. Whereas in his model the two sexes participate simultaneously and on an equal footing in the dignity of image of God, the apostle seems to teach a hierarchy: "Christ is the head of every man, man [i.e., the male individual] is the head of woman" (1 Cor. 11:3). The same male individual "is the image of God and reflects God's glory; but woman is the reflection of man's glory" (1 Cor. 11:7). The account of the creation of woman, taken from the man (Gen. 2:22), is then invoked in support of this assertion (1 Cor. 11:8-9). Paul thus justifies a custom—woman's wearing a veil and, later, the prohibition against women taking the floor to speak publicly in the Christian assemblies (1 Cor. 14:34-35). This argument is sometimes shocking, since it appears as an undissolved residue of masculine pride in Paul. But it is very interesting, if we under-stand that Scripture is not the didactic statement of a timeless system. Rather, it expresses a thought which, inspired though it is, remains human, striving to formulate itself in spite of the obstacles that it must surmount.

The account of the formation of woman, which Paul compares with the definition of man as the image of God, departs from the idea current in that society that woman is a subordinate being, and surpasses it by showing in the association of spouses a union closer than all other family ties. Likewise, the apostle is addressing a community where Jewish elements are without a doubt influential, and where the woman is held to be inferior. He does not wish to be curt

with that mentality, just as neither he nor the other
apostles will wish to suppress slavery immediately
(cf. 1 Pet. 2:18-25) before a new state of mind pene-
trates their hearts. He restricts himself for the time
being to remarking the mutual dependence of man
and woman in the transmission of life (1 Cor.
11:11-12). Elsewhere he will go further, teaching that
all differences of sex, culture, and social condition
are nothing in the Lord (Gal. 3:28; Col. 3:11): not
only have they no decisive importance for status in
the Kingdom of God, but in a community which
really clothes itself in the new man and which forces
itself to renewal in the image of its Creator (Col.
3:10), these differences should not occasion any
attempt to subjugate anyone, no matter who it might
be. Here again we find the notion of the image of
God, linked, as in Genesis 1:27, with the fundamental
equality of all.

For the moment, customs which he cannot replace
on the spot with better ones and which assure a
certain order in society should not be rejected
thoughtlessly: let the woman wear a veil. In the same
way, the old law forbade a man to wear women's
clothing and vice versa (Deut. 22:5). These specifica-
tions added by men's customs to the order established
by God deserve a certain respect, although they are
not absolute and unchangeable.

After these digressions around Genesis 1:27, it
would be well to restate what we have found, in order
to avoid overinterpretation. The formula of the first
creation account about male and female is concerned

first of all with the biological meaning of sexuality: fruitfulness. It says nothing explicitly about the psychological society between man and woman. But it clearly implies their fundamental equality as images of God.

[1]This idea is not necessarily false in itself, but it is not the one that the author of Genesis wished to impress upon his readers. It has been developed at length by the Protestant theologian Karl Barth, **Kirchliche Dogmatik,** III (1945), §41,2. Barth's views have been criticized by J. J. Stamm, **Die Imago-Lehre von Karl Barth und die alttestamentliche Wissenschaft,** pp. 84-98, in **Antwort: Karl Barth zum siebzigsten Geburtstag** (1956).

[2]Sirach 14:17-19. The noncanonical book of Enoch (15:4-7) developed this idea very systematically, helping us to understand an almost universal mentality.

[3]Ritual laws: Lev. 12; 15; 22:4; Num. 5:2; Deut. 23:11; cases of concrete application: Exod. 19:15; 1 Sam. 20:26; 21:5; 2 Sam. 11:4.

[4]"If God made us in His image, we have certainly paid Him back in kind."—Trans. note.

II

THE CREATION OF MAN
AND WOMAN (GEN. 2:4-25)

The Eden account, although older than the picture sketched by the hexaemeron, sees matters from a less universal viewpoint and has taken second place for this reason. But it contains a different outlook on the fact of sexuality. Instead of insisting primarily on fruitfulness (which is presumed rather than mentioned directly), this account sees the determining reason for woman's creation in the need for companionship.

Yahweh God formed man of dust from the soil, and made him a living being by the breath of life which He breathed into his nostrils. He placed him in the garden planted in Eden to work it and guard it. But, as if on second thought, He saw that it was not good for man to be alone, and so He decided to make him a suitable helpmate. But neither the beasts of the fields nor the birds of the air, which Yahweh God then fashioned from the earth, could serve as this helpmate. The man, watching them pass before him, could impose names on them—a symbol of the dominion he was to have over them—but he could not find in them the fellowship he sought. There is a lot of psychology hidden in this apparently naïve account. The man embarks first on a discovery of the world before he experiences the emotional need for conjugal companionship, whereas the woman immediately finds her destination in the man.

Yahweh forms the woman by removing from the sleeping man a portion of his body, a rib. He builds this rib into a woman, whom he presents to the man. The man recognizes in her what he vaguely desired, and, full of joy, he exclaims: "This at last is bone from my bones, / and flesh from my flesh: / This is to be called woman / for this was taken from man" (Gen. 2:23). There is a play on words, only somewhat translatable into English. By sheer chance, two words of different etymology, **ish** ("man") and **ishshah** ("woman"), agree as the masculine and feminine of the same word could agree in Hebrew. The storyteller is obviously not concerned with scientific linguistics, and he uses the assonance to underline the kinship of the two beings.

This symbolic text, which there is no reason to take literally, expresses remarkably the pre-eminent value of the conjugal society over all other social bonds. In the author's milieu the individual felt a close dependency on the group to which he belonged; ordinarily the family is the origin of all social units: clans, tribes, and nations were seen as enlarged families, descended from a single ancestor. Because of their common origin, all belonged to the same social "body"—and this was in no way understood metaphorically. People greeted one another by recognizing membership in the same body: "You are my bone

and flesh,"[1] the double expression serving in place of
a single more abstract word, as "organism" in English.
Thence flow duties of mutual aid and kindness. But
women are absent whenever the Bible uses the
expression. The author of the Eden account wishes
to affirm nevertheless that woman offers man a true
society. He therefore shows her issuing from man
and thus possessing the fundamental condition of
social union according to the ideas of ancient Israel,
namely, unity of physical origin. By adapting a traditional formula to the mutual relationship of spouses,
he wishes to place their union over and above the
bonds resulting from common ancestry.

In fact, the terms used, "bone from my bones,
flesh from my flesh," pun cleverly with the double
sense of the Hebrew preposition **min** ("from, from
out of"); indicating origin, it can also serve to express
the comparative degree, "more than." Thus the sense
can be either "body drawn from my body," or "relative closer than my close relatives."[2] The point of
the account is to make understood that no society is
as close and intimate as that of husband and wife.
As Ben Sirach will say later, "Friend or comrade—it is
always well met; / better than either, a wife and
husband" (Sirach 40:23). The formation of the couple
loosens prior bonds: "a man leaves his father and
mother and joins himself to his wife, and they become one body" (Gen. 2:24). The double formula
describes the conjugal union by its psychological aspects ("joins himself") and by its physical elements
("one body"). But it is not limited to this. In Hebrew

the term "body" or "flesh" does not necessarily have the primarily organic sense that it has in English; it can refer to the entire human being. Conjugal union of spouses is the beginning, the effective sign, the most intense moment of a common life which extends to all moments and areas of existence.

The **Symposium** of Plato, a similar account whose complicated burlesque contrasts with the sober restraint of Genesis, tries to explain homosexual as well as heterosexual tendencies. The biblical author would resolutely dismiss any suggestion of homosexuality that might arise. But this is not the only difference between Genesis and the **Symposium.**

Genesis does not present the notion of an androgynous being temporarily prior to the distinct sexes or ideally superior to them. While the **Symposium**'s ideas are reasonably clear in this direction, nothing suggests such an intention in the biblical account. Here the existence of separate sexes proceeds not from the god's jealousy of men's power, but from the Creator's goodness. Yahweh declares that it is not good that man should be alone, and He remedies his solitude by giving him a companion. Far from setting up total self-sufficiency as an ideal state, the narrator wishes to show that man is made for a life in society, in encounter. He uses the vocabulary of kinship and kindness and of the mutual aid which they involve. He takes issue with a social situation in which woman is an inferior and dependent being. This is why he shows her as drawn from the man and not created simultaneously with him, as the author of the hexaemeron was to do centuries later (as we have seen). He protests against the actual state of affairs, ascribing it to sin (Gen. 3:16), and finally comes to rank the affection of spouses above all other social bonds. The creation of woman gives man a good which he did not yet have. This is far from calling the duality of sexes a decay or at least a loss of a better condition, as the myth of a primal hermaphrodite would have it.

The attraction which pushes man and woman toward one another is not fate resulting from some prior state. It is comparable to, although more powerful than, the desire men have of entering into society with one another. Husband and wife become one body; that is, a single society based on affection is formed between them, as an alliance is sealed or renewed between men who recognize one another as their own flesh and bone. Sexual union makes manifestly real the entry of the two partners into a life of companionship. The word "love" is not used, but the reality implied by the remark that a man "joins himself" to the helpmate made for him by Yahweh is certainly very close to "love."

Unlike the **Symposium,** the Eden account does not explain the tendency of the two sexes to union in terms of desire to restore a prior unity but in terms of God's gift of the woman to the man. An explanation possible in a mythological account where men compete with the gods would result, in the setting of Genesis, in presenting conjugal union as opposition to the divine design: an attempt to reunite what God had separated. The biblical author's deep intention was revealed and clarified by Christ when He spoke of "what God has united" and what man must not dare to separate (Matt. 19:6). The ancient storyteller perhaps used a popular tale explaining the origin of sexual desire;[3] but if so, he noticeably softened the fanciful characteristics of his source, and turned it in a new direction: not limiting the affection of spouses to sexual union and showing the superiority of the couple's society over all others.

The account does not explicitly talk of fruitfulness. True, some have tried to discover it in the expression "they will become one body," i.e., in the infant born of their bodies.[4] But nothing in this account would prepare us for such a meaning; the New Testament did not find it: neither Christ implicitly (Matt. 19:5-6) nor St. Paul explicitly, in speaking of lustful union with a prostitute (1 Cor. 6:17).[5] Naturally the narrator would not for a moment think to exclude fruitfulness by silence; indeed he implies the notion everywhere.[6] The exemplary value of the Eden events is explicitly affirmed, because they concern the first ancestors of humanity. In the series of events resulting from sin, we find the divine sentence pronounced on the guilty woman, that she will give birth to her children in pain, and then the giving of the name "Eve" ("life"), chosen because she is the mother of all those who live (Gen. 3:16, 20). The inspired author, then, certainly does not forget that the child is the fruit of marriage. But—remarkable in a milieu so preoccupied with descendants—this text focuses its attention on the formation of a privileged society of man and woman. Such a characteristic foreshadows the Song of Songs.

[1]This expression is used for an uncle and a nephew (Gen. 29:14; 2 Sam. 19:14), for members of the same clan (Judg. 9:2), for members of the same tribe (2 Sam. 19:13), for members of the same people of Israel (2 Sam. 5:1; 1 Chron. 11:1). Judah says of his brother Joseph: "He is our brother, and our own flesh" (Gen. 37:27).

[2]This double sense has been pointed out by C. Hauret, **Origines Genese I-III** (1950), p. 103, n. 1.

[3]Cf. the data assembled in favor of this possible origin by A. H. Krappe, **The Birth of Eve**, pp. 312-322, in **Occident and Orient, Gaster Anniversary Volume**, ed. B. Schindler (1936). But it does not follow from the fact of borrowing that Genesis kept in fact the meaning of its models.

[4]Thus O. Procksch, **Die Genesis** (1913; G. von Rad, **Das erste Buch Mose** (1953); **Theologie des A. T.** (1957), Vol. I, p. 154.

[5]There is probably an allusion to the unity of the primitive human couple according to Gen. 2:23 in a somewhat obscure and variously interpreted text of Malachi (2:15). "Did God not create a single being that has flesh and the breath of life? And what is this single being destined for? God-given offspring" (translation of the Jerusalem Bible, inspired by A. van Hoonacker).

[6]Perhaps there is even an allusion to the future fruitfulness of the woman by a word-play in the use of the verb "to build" to describe her formation from the man's rib. In accounts literally close to the Eden account, this verb is used in the passive to express the possession of children (Gen. 16:2; 30:3). L. Ligier points out the comparison in **Peche d'Adam et peche du monde**, Vol. I (1960), pp. 243-244.

III.

THE ORDER OF NATURE
IN THE BIBLE

The fact of the duality of the sexes, then, is depicted in two ways, according to two different perspectives. The final redactor juxtaposed the two accounts without attempting to resolve their differences or to judge the value of their data. In the one, biological fruitfulness is emphasized; in the other, the society of man and woman—a society of love according to the divine intention, but in fact of enslavement of woman, after the sin.

This teaching of Genesis 1-3 sums up what might be called an "order of nature." Though not literally biblical, this phrase is close to many scriptural expressions. It can, however, lead to difficulties; some clarification is therefore necessary. It concerns an order established by God in creation; universally valid, not restricted to a limited group; permanent and enduring, at least in substance, despite the perversion of men; corresponding to the nature of creatures since the creation, not the fruit of some contingent historical institution (as rites would be, for instance); finally, recognizable even outside the chosen people, not always requiring positive revelation for at least partial discovery.

The biblical authors had a feeling for cosmic harmony. They saw the different parts of the world as organically linked; a disorder introduced by man provokes a reaction from all creation. They often express their view in colorful anthropomorphic terms: the heavens shudder with indignation at human perversity (Jer. 2:12); the land vomits out its inhabitants who disgust it by their sexual dissoluteness (Lev. 18:15, 28; 20:22). Sometimes too the thought becomes more rational.[1] Jeremiah speaks of the "laws" of the sun, moon, and stars, which assure the regular succession of day and night (Jer. 31:35-36; cf. 33:25), and of the different seasons of the year which stand as a law for agricultural work (Jer. 5:24; cf. Gen. 8:22). The psalmist contemplates with admiration the visible world, wherein God's wisdom is seen disposing all things to satisfy His creatures' needs (Ps. 104).

This order fascinates man when he tries to look at it; but it carries unfathomable depths, which a creature must not hope to penetrate—as Job is forced to acknowledge when Yahweh himself presses him with a series of unanswerable questions (Job 38-41). Among the marvels which surpass the reach of intelligence are numbered the formation of a child in his mother's womb (Ps. 139:13-15; Eccles. 11:5; 2 Macc. 7:22) and the attraction of a man for a girl (Prov. 30:19). The natural order, despite its goodness, is somewhat deceiving: everything in it begins over and over again indefinitely—cycles of seasons and of physical phenomena, human generations which are born to die—and no one can ever observe the lasting

result. This Qoheleth calls vanity, and his experience
of it is a bitter one (Eccles. 1:2-11). This view is still
somewhat short-sighted; St. Paul will compliment it
with a source of hope: the condition of the creature
subject to vanity and decadence is only temporary;
it is in line with the actual situation of men subject
to a test, and it will give way to complete perfection
in freedom and glory (Rom. 8:19-24). The practical
consequence of this is that the ordinary run of things
should not be considered as determining in all circumstances a rigid rule of human conduct: God's
grace can at times enable man to anticipate the
future goal as, for example, in the case of celibacy
chosen for the sake of the kingdom of heaven (Matt.
19:12).

In the Bible, religious faith and in particular the
beliefs coming from the election and deliverance of
Israel deeply penetrate knowledge of the order of
nature. Beginning from a situation established by the
alliance—hope of numerous progeny, possession of a
country, respect for the weak—the inspired authors
strive to distinguish, in the brute data of experience,
what corresponds to a creative will and what results
from the guilt of men. But pagan peoples too have a
certain appreciation of moral good and evil, and they
can sometimes see with indignation and disgust the
depravity of the people of God who have fallen back
into sin (Ezek. 16:27).

The opening chapters of Genesis take a first inventory of the order of nature. They trace, in fact,

the major lines of the human condition, showing how
they form an integral part of the world and yet
bringing everything back to the will of God, Author
of heaven and earth. This picture applies to all men.
Later the author will attempt to enumerate the sub-
divisions of the human family, before focusing exclusively on the race of Abraham (Gen. 10). He does not
lose interest in humanity as a whole even then, since
he announces that all men will be blessed in Abraham
(Gen. 12:3; 18:18; 22:18). What is said in the creation
accounts concerns all men and thus differs from
ritual prescriptions such as circumcision or the bloody
sacrifices that will be imposed on the patriarchs and
on Moses.

The divine plan realized in creation is definitive.
The flood, recounted at length in Genesis 6-8, repre-
sents the threat of total destruction of the divine work
by a just punishment. But in His merciful wisdom,
God simply eliminates the perversions introduced by
human malice. The blessings bestowed on Noah after
the cataclysm only take up again the themes of the
blessing which had followed creation: fruitfulness and
domination of the earth. Fine nuances refer to the
fact that, in a world where sin has entered, complete
primal harmony no longer exists. Man's mastery
over animals is now imposed by fear and terror;
the use of animal flesh is added to vegetal food, an
indication of the violence which disturbed the original
peace (Gen. 9:1-7). In the same way, the divine
sentence following the fall had already announced
that, from then on, the mutual attraction of man

and woman would be accompanied by a painful subjection of the latter (Gen. 3:16).

Thus the order of creation remains, although burdened with certain changes; the lines traced by Genesis 1 and 2 are recognizable, at least partially, in the data of experience. It is not a question of an ideal totally lost since then. The distinction of male and female and the fruitfulness that results from their union obviously remain, as does the constitution of a new society, the couple, of man and woman, which loosens the prior bond of the child to his parents. What exists and is observed in reality, then, results simultaneously from a good will and from a perverse will of man, who can change in part the divine work. Israel, despite her strong feeling of free election by God—thus of an initiative limited to one human group and independent of the qualities of this small people —did not have her eyes closed to the order of nature.

Different passages in the prophets and the wisdom books testify to this, but the creation accounts in Genesis represent the most compact exposé of the order of nature. The biblical authors have no thought of canonizing everything that actually happens; they are perfectly aware that there are disorders in the world. They tried to draw a partial distinction between what is good, because established by God, and what is bad, because degraded by sin. Even if they sometimes offer man the example of animal behavior (Isa. 1:3; Jer. 8:7; Prov. 6:6), they never forget what distinguishes man from animal and constitutes his inalienable superiority: the image of God.

In the very context where he refers to this notion of the divine image, St. Paul stigmatizes pagan homosexuality as "unnatural" (Rom. 1:26-27). While he does not fully elaborate a concept of the order of nature within revelation, he condemns as especially serious the disorder represented by the exercise of sexuality outside of relations between man and woman. Similarly, the Old Testament had condemned bestiality (Exod. 22:18; Lev. 18:23; 20:15-16; Deut. 27:21), implicitly agreeing with the Genesis idea of man, which said that among the animals no helpmate had been found suitable for man.

What a Christian should note particularly is Christ's recourse to the order of nature expressed in the creation accounts. When presented with the question of divorce, Jesus consecrates the concept of sexuality and marriage contained in the texts, declares them of more lasting value than the temporary accommodations made by the law of Moses, and gives them as the rules according to which problems of conduct should be resolved from then on.

In His answer to the Pharisees who interrogate Him about the reasons capable of legitimating divorce, the Master quotes the formula of the hexaemeron, "He made them male and female," then the lines which draw the moral of the story of the formation of woman, "This is why a man must leave father and mother, and cling to his wife, and the two become one body" (Matt. 19:3-9). The distinction of the sexes is the work of God, but so is their stable union in marriage. To dissolve this society would be to go

against the will of God. There is no question here of
the child; Christ's answer holds true for all marriages,
not only for actually fruitful ones. But it is true
that the answer is phrased in view of the question.
Jesus does not mean by His silence to declare periph-
eral or secondary the views of the inspired book on
fruitfulness at the very moment when He consecrates
its authority and invites the Pharisees to find in it
the expression of the Creator's permanent design.
But He does show that the union of spouses already
has a value in itself, even before being blessed with
offspring.

The Christian knows that the law and the prophets
have been completed, not abolished, by his Lord
(Matt. 5:17). He can welcome the notion of an order
of nature suggested by the Old Testament. Despite
the absence of the word itself, he need not see the
idea as an irrelevant speculation which interferes
with the divine message. With Christ, he recognizes
in Genesis 1-2 the major lines of the order established
by God; but not being superstitiously servile to the
letter of the text, he is open to what more careful
observation can discover of the details of a reality
already recognized and judged in essence. He can
welcome the data of the modern human sciences, not
to discover completely original religious and moral
values in them, but to profit from a more complete
inventory of the potentialities of creation.

[1]On this approach to the idea of the order of nature in the
Old Testament, cf. W. Eichrodt, **Theologie des Alten Testaments,** Vol. II (1935; second edition, 1961), §17, 1; F. Horst
Naturrecht und das Alte Testament, in **Evang. Theologie,** 10
(1950), pp. 253-273 (reprinted in **Gottes Recht** [1961], pp.
235-259).

IV

THE DOUBLE PERSPECTIVE:
LOVE AND FRUITFULNESS

The whole Old Testament reflects the twofold aspect of the teaching on sexuality presented by the creation accounts. It could be said in general that the desire for descendants appears dominant in most of the texts that speak of marriage.[1] The blessing bestowed on mankind at the beginning, fruitfulness and domination of the earth, is the one that the patriarchs receive anew in their distress. The ancestors of Israel, wandering far from their fatherland and having the sterility of old age, obtain at last by a divine promise received in faith that which they so ardently desired: descendants as numerous as the stars of heaven, and a land (Gen. 15:5-7). This reprise in a minor key of the magnificent blessing of the creation account clearly shows the importance which the author of Genesis accords to it. The lesson is not the last: the law extends the promise to the whole people (Lev. 26:9; Deut. 28:11); the psalmists in their turn sing of the divine favor of being crowned with sons (Ps. 112:2; 127; 128).

Perhaps the experience of marriage, often bitter in those times of polygamy and divorce, led the biblical authors to insist more heavily upon what was a pledge of hope: posterity, the condition for God's future blessing on His people. Jeremiah counsels his contemporaries in exile in Babylon to marry and to choose spouses for their children, to increase, and to turn to agriculture (Jer. 29:6).

The wisdom writers, too, extol the happiness of having children (Prov. 17:6; Sirach 30:1-6), but they strongly instill the duty to look after their education. This is the indispensable condition for some day finding joy in one's descendants. The methods anticipated are energetic. The father of the family should not spare the rod (Prov. 19:18; 23:13-14; 29:17). His inspiration in this is a firm and foreseeing love (Prov. 13:24), preferable to an affection too soft. David had not dared to reprimand his heir apparent (1 Kings 1:6); the results were cabals and intrigues that ended in blood (1 Kings 2:23-25). The maxims of wisdom also exhort parents to show themselves severe when necessary (Prov. 20:30; 29:15; Sirach 7:23; 30:1-13), for the child's heart needs to be rid of his folly (Prov. 22:15). The mother should bear her share of this educative task (Prov. 1:8; 4:3; 31:1). Tobit is a perfect model of paternal solicitude which is rewarded at last. The duty of correction went so far that the law enjoined parents themselves to deliver a debauched and obstinately rebellious son to capital punishment (Deut. 21:18-21). This must have been an extreme and rare case, but it emphasizes the seriousness that characterized the duty of education. The simple fact is that, for Israel, it was a question

of transmitting divine revelation (Gen. 18:19), the
pledge of national survival (Ps. 77:3-8).

In the writings of the last centuries before Christ,
the concern for moral and religious excellence is so
strong as to prefer childlessness to criminal descendants (Sirach 16:1-3; Wisdom 3:13-14; 4:1-6). A eunuch
was excluded by law from the holy community of
the Chosen People, yet a late prophet promised him
a name better than sons and daughters (Isa. 56:3-5).
Thus was overcome the feeling, so deeply rooted in
the heart at that time, that there was no greater grief
than to be deprived of a natural heir (Gen. 15:3).

The narrative books brought together some accounts in which marriages contracted in obedience
to God's will and that of the parents brought love
and happiness to the spouses. Rebekah, the fiancée
pointed out by a providential sign to the servant who
traveled a great distance to fetch her, is brought to
Isaac; the young man, though he did not choose her
himself, marries her, loves her, and so was consoled
at the death of his mother (Gen. 24:67). The story of
Tobias was undoubtedly inspired by this patriarchial
model. When he learns that Sirach is his kinswoman,
destined for him by virtue of the Mosaic law, Tobias
falls in love with her before meeting her, and gives
her his heart (Tobit 6:18). After the marriage has
been contracted, Tobias prays, recalling the Creator's
providential design according to Genesis: Eve created
to be the man's help and giving birth to the whole
human race, for it is not good that the man should
be alone (Tobit 8:6).

In these two examples the spouses love each other because they are married. But there are also cases where passion precedes and leads to marriage. Jacob falls in love with his beautiful cousin Rachel and agrees to work for Laban for seven years in order to win her as his wife (Gen. 29:11-30). Samson chooses a Philistine maiden and cannot be dissuaded from his love by the remonstrances of his parents (Judg. 14:1-3). Michal, daughter of King Saul, falls in love with the young leader David; here, remarkably, the initiative comes from the feminine side (1 Sam. 18:20).

These few marriages of love probably stood as exceptions, noted precisely because of their rarity, at least in ancient times. Various texts from the narrative, prophetic, and wisdom books report as self-evident the fact that the father gives his daughter (or brothers their sister) in marriage, with hardly any inquiry into the girl's feelings.[2] In the case of Rebekah, her consent does not bear on the marriage itself, which is already settled, but on the immediacy of the departure for the new and distant family (Gen. 24:55-58). The parents ordinarily intervene even for a son (Gen. 21:21; 24:1-4; Exod. 34:16). This must have been the general custom at a time when the great concern was to continue the family line and when individual rights took second place. The biblical texts cited do not intend to present a praiseworthy example for imitation; they simply reflect the facts. If any rule is to be found (a directive indication, that is; not a rigorous prescription), we must look for it in

the Song of Songs. There, as we will see later, the
eager longing of the lovers strains toward permanent
union—toward marriage.

The law protected the union of a newly married
couple. A fiancé was exempted from participating
in a military campaign (Deut. 20:7). For one year
the young husband was free from all military obli-
gations and other business, "to bring joy to the wife
he has taken" (Deut. 24:5).

The wisdom books saw God's favor in the happiness which a wife gives to her husband (Prov. 18:22;
19:14; Eccles. 9:9; Sirach 26:1-4; 26:13-18). They often
praised faithful conjugal love without explicitly mentioning children, of whom they spoke in other passages (Prov. 11:16; 12:4; Sirach 7:19; 36:21-27; 40:23).
A short lyric poem, while an exhortation to fidelity,
recalls something of the impassioned lines of the
Song of Songs:

> Find joy with the wife you married
>   in your youth,
> fair as a hind, graceful as a fawn.
> Let hers be the company you keep,
>   hers the breasts that ever fill you
>   with delight,
>   hers the love that ever holds you captive.
> Why be seduced, my son, by an alien woman,
> and fondle the breast of a woman who
>   is a stranger?
>
> Proverbs 5:18-20

The prophet Ezekiel uses a comparable expression
when, at his wife's death, he calls her "the delight

of his eyes" (Ezek. 24:16). If the prophet is then obliged to refrain from all exterior show of mourning, it is not by insensibility but because his mission to carry God's Word has a total claim on him. He must not only proclaim the divine judgment by his words, but prefigure it by his actions: the coming catastrophe will not even leave men the leisure to lament the dead. By Yahweh's order Jeremiah likewise had to renounce founding a home in order to announce the calamity of the exile, which would overthrow all families (Jer. 16:1-8).

Notably, the Old Testament does not seem to have arrived at a unified view of conjugal love and the happiness of a fruitful home. The only word of tenderness between spouses is spoken by Elkanah to his still-barren wife: "Hannan, am I not more to you than ten sons?" (1 Sam. 1:8). In the poem on the perfect wife, what corresponds to the sons' admiration for their mother is the husband's solid esteem for the companion of his life and the manager of his household, rather than a sentimental affection (Prov. 31:11-28). Love appears in the Old Testament like a flower which prepares the fruitfulness of the plant and disappears when it is assured. This will change in the New Testament, which seems to look more positively on the coexistence of diverse familial values.

¹The Bible does not directly consider the modern problems of relative birth control and the methods, legitimate or not, used for this purpose. Onan (Gen. 38:8-10) is guilty of an absolute refusal of all fatherhood, and this in a very special case: that of a Levirate marriage (the marriage of a brother-in-

law with his childless, widowed sister-in-law), where the decisive reason for the new union and its essential consideration was the begetting of children destined to be the legal heirs of the deceased first husband. In such circumstances, voluntarily sterility was a treacherous fraud. **Coitus interruptus,** which Onan used, was known in Israel; but it was not the object of rigorous legal prohibition, as were homosexuality (Lev. 18:22; 20:13) and bestiality (Exod. 22:18; Lev. 18:23; 20:15-16; Deut. 27:21). The law was therefore concerned with restricting sexual activity to relations between man and woman, but it did not explicitly prohibit the sterility of a marriage. Fruitfulness was undoubtedly taken for granted in most cases, and moreover was not considered the unique end of marriage.

[2]Here are some examples, not an exhaustive list: Gen. 29:23-27; 34:8-17; Exod. 2:21; Judg. 1:12; 1 Sam. 18:17-21; 1 Chron. 2:35; Jer. 29:6; Tobit 7:11; Sirach 7:25; 36:21.

V.

LOVE IN THE
SONG OF SONGS

Far surpassing all other texts as a celebration of conjugal love, the Song of Songs is a love poem in which two betrothed persons or young spouses express their mutual tenderness, desire, and admiration. Such is the obvious meaning, and there is no solid reason to attribute to the author a symbolic intention: representing, as did the prophets, the mutual love of God and His people.[1] This poem, apparently completely worldly, only mentions the divine name in an idiomatic metaphor ("flame of Yahweh," Song 8:6—the lightning flash) which overuse had probably rendered trite. Yet it entered the collection of the Scriptures of Israel. It must have been an old and valued piece of literature conserved at a time when concern for the heritage of the past was great, such as the period of restoration by Nehemiah after the Babylonian exile (2 Macc. 2:13) or under the government of Judas Maccabaeus after the persecution of Antiochus Epiphanes (cf. 2 Macc. 2:14).

Not all the festivities celebrated by Israel had a religious character: such was the festival where the maidens came out to dance in the vineyards (Judg.

21:21) or the annual lamentations for the daughter of Jephthah, sacrificed before having known marriage or motherhood (Judg. 11:40). Besides the noise of the millstone and the light of the lamp, Jeremiah the prophet lists among the normal manifestations of a happy existence the cries of rejoicing and mirth, the voice of the fiancé and the fiancée—all of which will disappear at the coming exile (Jer. 7:34; 16:9; 25:10; cf. Lam. 5:14-15; Ps. 78:63), but which will be re-established at the return from captivity (Jer. 33:11). The "voice of the fiancé and the fiancée" refers either to songs sung by them at their marriage celebrations or to songs expressing their mutual feelings and liable to be found, in different circumstances, on the lips of professional and nonprofessional singers. Ezekiel tells us that his contemporaries greatly enjoyed these love songs when the music was accompanied by a beautiful voice (Ezek. 33:22; cf. Sirach 40:21). Simon ben Gamaliel, a Jewish rabbi of the second century of our era, recalls nostalgically a joyous custom observed before the destruction of the Temple by the Romans in A.D. 70: maidens dressed in white came out of Jerusalem and went into the vineyards, where they invited the young men to choose a fiancée according to their tastes; the maidens sang alternately the poem on the perfect wife (Prov. 31:30-31) and the couplet of the wedding of Solomon in Song 3:11.[2]

It follows from these testimonies that the people of Israel had long enjoyed the singing of love poems. It was only normal, then, that written collections

would be drawn up to aid the memories of professional and nonprofessional singers—as we see happen
with the love lyric in Egypt and with other genres
of poetry in Israel. Nevertheless, poetic quality was
insufficient to warrant automatic acceptance into the
collection of books considered inspired by God.
Israel did not confuse poetic inspiration with the
biblical inspiration that made a writing the bearer of
God's Word. Here and there in the Bible we find
quotations from various books that have not been
integrally preserved for us: war epics (Num. 21:14-15,
27-30; Josh. 10:12-13; cf. Num. 21:17-18), dirges (2
Sam. 1:19-27; 2 Chron. 35:25), liturgical hymns (1
Kings 8:12-13).

That the small book the Song of Songs has come
down to us in the biblical collection is not simply
because of a connection to some custom deeply
rooted in the people's hearts and lives; this had not
sufficed to preserve the lament for Josiah (2 Chron.
35:25). There has to be the more or less conscious
recognition of a positive value in it— the expression
of love as God wills it. Just as the psalter teaches
how to pray without giving a course on prayer, so
the poems of the Song of Songs, recited in various
situations in profane life, taught young men and
women what a genuine love should be. And they
did so more persuasively and effectively than could
theoretical advice. Israel found in the Song of Songs
the education in love which today we can look for
more or less satisfactorily in popular films, novels,
and songs. Love is a natural emotion, i.e., correspond-

ing to what man is, such as God created him; but it
needs to be educated by the communication of
another's experiences, as do so many other natural
activities.

We are sometimes tempted to think that the
human context of the Song of Songs is clear and that
there is no need for an inspired writing to teach it
to the Chosen People. Yet comparison with other
love songs of the ancient East brings significant differences into relief alongside the great similarities.
Above all, Israel's general state of mind, which was
so strongly convinced of the obligation to continue
the race and which thus centered almost exclusively
upon this function of fruitfulness in marriage, found
a very opportune corrective in the Song of Songs.
Better than a law often tolerant toward hardness of
heart (Matt. 19:8), better than the prophets or the
wisdom writers, the biblical poem expressed certain
demands of the heart that have become, if not in all
cases a strict Christian law, at least the components
of a Christian ideal of marriage. It is useful then to
undertake the unpleasant task of saying in prose
what has been sung in such inimitable poetry. Without stopping to consider numerous obscure details,
we can clarify many sure points.

First of all, in a milieu that admitted polygamy,
the love celebrated by the Song of Songs is unique.
The lover contrasts his unique fiancée, a faultless
love, to the large harem of the king (Song 6:8-9).
Far from feeling disadvantaged, he finds in her a
unique treasure of incomparable value, summing up

in itself all the riches of the visible world, the
splendors of the stars, the charms of nature, the
grace of gazelles, and the sumptuousness of flowers
in springtime. From these arise his enthusiastic
descriptions (4:1-15; 6:4-10; 7:2-10), which are not left
unanswered:

> My beloved is fresh and ruddy,
> to be known among ten thousand.
> > Song of Songs 5:10

Not only does the matrimonial institution become
monogamous, but the feeling experienced by the
lovers is marvelously intensified by this unification
and is enabled to see the inimitable in the person of
the beloved:

> —As a lily among the thistles,
> so is my love among the maidens.

> —As an apple tree among the trees
> > of the orchard,
> so is my Beloved among the young men.
> > Song of Songs 2:2-3

In a milieu that admitted divorce, the love of
the Song of Songs foresees no end. Just before the
conclusion of the poem, the maiden or the young
wife addresses an impassioned prayer to her beloved:

> Set me like a seal on your heart,
> like a seal on your arm.
> For love is strong as Death,
> jealousy relentless as Sheol.
> The flash of it is a flash of fire,

a flame of Yahweh himself.
Love no flood can quench,
no torrents drown.
                    Song of Songs 8:6-7

Love must impress the indelible image of the
beloved on the lover's heart, and avert any desire
which might lead toward someone else. It is as
irrevocable as the entry into death, the country
from which no one returns. It is always able to find
new nourishment, like the insatiable fire (Prov. 30:16).
It is an invincible force, like the lightning bolt. It is
stronger than unforeseen adversity (symbolized by
the inundation).

In a milieu where paternal authority was usually
the only determining factor in a daughter's marriage,
the love of the Song of Songs is free and comes from
a choice made by the girl herself. This, it seems, is
the meaning of the lines where the girl protests
against the dominance her brothers wish to exercise
over her. They had made her look after the vineyards and she has not looked after her own (Song
1:6). The detail is somewhat obscure and can be
clarified in different ways, but the intention can
hardly be debated. The young girl will not agree
to submit herself absolutely to her brothers' orders
when it is a question of looking for her beloved.
Likewise she refuses her brothers' pretensions to
dispose of her marriage. She scoffs at their self-
seeking calculations about the dowry they will demand of a future husband (Song 8:8-10). It would
have been shocking to raise this accusation against

the father, but the brothers could be mocked without
exposing the satire to censorship. Thus the ideal of a
free love springing from the partners instead of a
union dictated by social considerations entered Israel
by a roundabout way.

In a milieu where woman was readily considered
inferior, where she did not enjoy the same social
rights as the man, the two partners of the Song of
Songs are on a perfectly equal footing. After the fall,
the divine sentence had expressed the dependent
condition of the wife: "Your yearning shall be for
your husband, yet he will lord it over you" (Gen.
3:16). Love freed the fiancée from this servitude:

> I am my Beloved's,
> and his desire is for me.
> Song of Songs 7:11

It is obviously not a question of the ownership by
which a married woman was considered one subject
among the rest in the husband's house, on a level
with his slaves and his domestic animals (Exod. 20:17).
The belonging is mutual and, presumably, freely
agreed to: "My Beloved is mine and I am his." Thus
the search too is mutual: the beloved comes to visit
his fiancée (Song 2:9; 5:2-3), and the maiden seeks
him in the country (Song 1:7) or in the city during
the night (Song 3:1-4; 5:4-8). Their admiration is
reciprocal. The poem contains two or three enthusiastic descriptions of feminine beauty (Song 4:1-5;
6:4-7, 10; 7:1-7), a common literary form in the
ancient East; but it contains something much less

common as well—a corresponding description of masculine beauty (5:10-16). Thus the Song of Songs stands as the clearest witness to, and probably the agent of, a promotion of woman, a promotion whose indications can be noted throughout the Old Testament.

The love hymned by this biblical poem is esteemed beyond all things: it is without price. After an ardent call to fidelity, this aphorism appears: "Were a man to offer all the wealth of his house to buy love, contempt is all he would purchase" (Song 8:7). How vile the man who would believe himself able to buy love for money (cf. Acts 8:20)! The sentence has sometimes been understood interrogatively: Who would despise the impassioned lover who, in order to have his beloved, would pay a greedy family a disproportionate dowry? The thought is the same, expressed in a different form. What follows continues the same theme. The maiden recalls in a mocking tone of voice that such bargaining was not unknown (Song 8:9). But the young man takes the floor and declares that he prefers his own vine—meaning his beautiful one—to the rich vineyards of Solomon (Song 8:11-12; cf. Ps. 128:3).

This love fills the heart, dispenses the greatest joys. Although its description is somewhat idealized, this love is not utopian. Often it lives not in full possession of the other, but in waiting, in yearning, in desolate search. Two scenes, variations on the same theme, show us the maiden wandering the city at night in search of her beloved, who is absent or has suddenly disappeared (Song 3:1-4; 5:2-8). The second is particularly significant: it is in separation that passion reaches its full intensity. Is the account a dream, which would explain the somewhat unusual situations and the rapid turn of events? Is it a poetic fiction, imagining dramatic circumstances to give free rein to emotion? Is the negative response of the young girl (Song 5:3) a lover's tease, but one which provokes unforeseen misunderstanding and the resentment of her suitor? Is it a lack of eagerness justly punished? In any case, the rapid disappearance of her beloved reduces the maiden almost to despair; thereafter she is able to brave many obstacles. Love then is not simply idle happiness; it is the source of sufferings and pains which must be faced courageously (cf. Song 8:7).

The yearning depicted in the Song of Songs is not disincarnated. The two lovers extol with neither prudishness nor excess their physical charms and the caresses that they exchange. Some have occasionally judged these descriptions too sensual, or been stunned at their presence in the collection of Scripture. This alleged anomaly was explained in different ways: inattention on the part of those in charge of the canonical collection, violent allegorization after the fact, the poet's symbolic intention. But we must remember that in Genesis (2:24) marital union was already implicit in the general formula explaining woman's creation. True, the Song of Songs is more emphatic; as such, it can help us to a greater awareness of this human situation which has been consecrated by its

entry into the Christian sacramental economy. "Car
le surnaturel est lui-même charnel."[3] It is impossible
to distinguish two domains in man that touch one
another superficially without interpenetrating. In love,
the attachment of the heart and the attraction of the
senses come together and support and strengthen one
another. The Song of Songs expresses healthy emotion
very different from the morbid fate binding Tristan
and Iseult in a passion that, if it remains chaste, is
realized only in death. In conformity with the general
conviction of Israel's faith that life is a gift of God,
the bodily is not forgotten or suppressed in the
biblical poem. But it is never simply equivalent to
the satisfaction of a selfish desire; it is always subordinate to a tenderness addressed to the person.
One indication of this is that the love of the two
partners is never compared to animal oestrus; the
same reserve is not found in reasonably similar
bucolic poems, such as those of Theocritus, Virgil, or
Ronsard. Love in the Song of Songs never descends
to an animal level. In this small book so filled with
nature, flocks, and flowered pastures, love keeps
its distinctive human character as a free gift of persons. It has not been kept immersed to the point of
dissolution in the flood of sensuality which the
myths and rites of the pagan East celebrated as
involving the gods, men, and animal and vegetable
life in a cycle of death and rebirth. Love simply
opened the lovers' eyes to everything gracious, sweet,
charming, and pleasant in the visible world. Whereas
biblical poets like those of Psalms and of Job were
sensitive to the redoubtable and grandiose aspects of

creatures in order to find in them the reflection of
a terrible, holy, and judging God, the poet of the
Song of Songs composed a hymn to the very good
creation of the beginning (Gen. 1:31). He does not
name the creator, but he loves and admires his whole
work. There is hardly anything comparable in this
regard except the Gospel, with its touching attention
to the sumptuous adornment of the wild flowers
(Matt. 6:28).

Unlike other epithalamia whose tenor the Bible
preserved (Gen. 24:60; Ruth 4:11-12; Ps. 45:17), the
love songs we are considering do not mention the
bride's future fruitfulness, though they imply it
throughout. Admiration for the life of nature, for
the springtime awakening of vegetation, for the
flocks, for the gazelle followed by her twin fawns
(Song 4:5; 7:4) is incompatible with a rejection of
fruitfulness. The fiancée is compared to a vine (Song
8:12), the psalmist's image of the wife-mother (Ps.
128:3; cf. Ezek. 19:10). The only marriage mentioned
is that of Solomon (Song 3:11); more than any other,
the royal union must be fruitful to assure the dynastic
succession (Ps. 45:17). There is probably an allusion
to motherhood in the mention of mandrakes (Song
7:14), which were thought to avert sterility (Gen.
30:14-16). The fiancé meets his beloved at the very
place where her mother conceived her (Song 8:5):
this is to suggest that she in her turn will become a
mother. The Song of Songs therefore depicts a love
that participates without reserve in the great current
of life in expansion. It develops almost exclusively

the emotional aspect of union between man and woman, but without creating a Malthusian atmosphere. It is very much in line with the account of woman's creation (Gen. 2:18-24). Both texts insist on the partners' mutual affection; and yet, far from excluding fruitfulness, they both rather clearly imply it.

These love poems remain constantly in a purely human context. They are never even briefly marked by a religious expression that would place the lovers' union under the divine law and safeguard. The "flame of Yahweh" (Song 8:6) is probably only a trite metaphor for "lightning bolt," which has lost all properly religious dimension, like "act of God" in English. Certainly this constitutes a lacuna in the Song of Songs by comparison with a Christian text like Ephesians 5:22-33. But unless we disregard time and history, we must recognize this as a general characteristic of the Old Testament, where values that will be synthesized in the Christian message still remain unorganized and separated from one another.

This silence is nevertheless not without positive import. By not confusing the Creator and the creature, it testifies to the transcendence of God in its own way. Living in the midst of the ancient East, Israel was surrounded by pagan religions that attributed to the divine world the same duality of sexes observable in men and in animals. Everything was subject to the same law of sensual desire and of fruitfulness. The biblical love songs manifest Yahwism's break with these ideas, and there are other witnesses as well. According to the prophets, Yahweh has no sex; He maintains a quasi-nuptial alliance with His Chosen People and not with a goddess consort. According to the account of the six days of creation (Gen. 1), God produced the world by His word alone, but animals and men reproduce themselves by sexual union. According to the account of woman's creation (Gen. 2:18-25), sexual distinction in mankind is not limited to the procreative end. Between man and woman exists an association closer than any other family bond. The Song of Songs develops this teaching in poetry; it exalts the love of a human couple far above the mating of animals. But it does not speak of Yahweh, who is above all sexuality. To mention Him in songs consecrated to the tenderness of man and woman and probably indebted to the literary forms of pagan poetry would have been to risk a terrible misunderstanding even in Israel, where the sensual mythology of surrounding polytheism was not entirely unknown. The danger was that, instead of making love holy, one would consign or even debase Yahweh to the level of the pagan gods, His still-dangerous rivals for the hearts of the people.

Considered in its historical setting, the silence observed by the Song of Songs with regard to God is an indirect homage to His transcendence. It avoided not only the superficial profanation of pronouncing the sacred name in a context of worldly rejoicing (there is a like omission in the scroll of Esther), but also the infinitely more serious profana-

tion of exposing the infinite perfection of the Creator
to misjudgment.[4] It marks therefore a necessary step
in the progress of the full revelation; it undertook an
energetic purification of love, by destroying all the
ambiguous contaminations from a notion that con-
fused the divine with a sexuality which, when it was
not perverted, remained too animal. Later on, the
New Testament will be able to accomplish a new
sanctification of love. But the amorous dialogues of
the Song of Songs already show us how much the
Chosen People's encounter with the living God had
been able to ennoble the encounter between human
persons.

[1]For an expose of the different interpretations of the Song
of Songs and a critique of the religious allegorical interpreta-
tion, cf. A. M. Dubarle, **L'amour humain dans Le Cantique
des Cantiques**, in **Revue Biblique** 61 (1954), pp. 67-86; **Le
Cantique des Cantiques dans l'exegese recente** (conference at
the Journees Biblique at Louvain, August, 1963), in **Recherches
Bibliques**, VIII: **Aux grands carrefours de la revelation et de
l'exergese de l'Ancien Testament** (1967), pp. 139-152; J. P.
Audet, **Le sens du Cantique des Cantiques**, in **Revue Biblique**
62 (1955), pp. 197-221. I will not bring these discussions up
in this context.

[2]Text cited by M. H. Segal, **The Song of Songs**, in **Vetus
Testamentum** 12 (1962), pp. 470-490; cf. p. 485.

[3]C. Peguy, **Eve** (1847); **Oeuvres completes**, N.R.F., Vol.
VII, p. 182. ("For the supernatural is itself flesh."—Trans.
note.)

[4]In ancient Egyptian love poetry there are a good number
of prayers to the gods asking that they might favor the wishes
of the lovers. There is even a passage (of somewhat uncertain
translation) where the young girl, comparing the sweetest
flavors to gall and salt by contrast with her beloved, declares
that to possess him is to possess the god Amon; cf. P. Gilbert,
La poesie egyptienne (second edition, 1949), pp. 54-55.

VI

THE ILLS OF LOVE

The concrete experience of love was not always happy. Qoheleth sums up a feeling which seems to have been common among the wisdom writers: "I find woman more bitter than death; she is a snare, her heart a net, her arms are chains" (Eccles 7:26).

Is Qoheleth referring to woman in general or to a specific category of women? The grammar cannot give an answer, and it is the reader's intimate feeling that must decide.

Many passages recount a love which turns out badly. Jacob felt a great love for Rachel, but she is given to him in marriage only after her older sister, Leah, has taken her place by trickery. The favorite wife remains barren and becomes despondent. This offers a chance for the neglected wife to hope again for her husband's affection. The two sisters compete and give their servants to Jacob as concubines, in order to increase their offspring (Gen. 29:15-30:24). A family life begun under apparently happy auspices is troubled by dissensions, even though Leah and Rachel were later honored as having built the house of Israel (Ruth 4:11).

Samson, a hero of the guerrillas of independence

against the Philistine domination, is the victim of his love for foreign women. His first wife, whom he had married out of passion, gave in to the threats of her compatriots. By plaintive entreaties she wheedles from her husband the answer to a riddle proposed on a bet, and she hurries to divulge it. Samson, obliged to pay off the wager, makes the best of it by massacring some Philistines (Judg. 14:12-20). He later marries another woman, Delilah, who, this time out of greed, importunes him with her questions until he reveals the source of his prodigious strength; she uses this knowledge to betray him to his enemies, who put out his eyes (Judg. 16:4-21). These stories undoubtedly intend to warn against mixed marriages: the foreign wife was ready to betray her husband, because she valued the original community of blood more than the bond created by marriage. But they contain a more general teaching as well: love may not always be mutual; in such a case it betrays the lover into the hands of the object of his passion.

Thus did David seduce Bathsheba. The king of a large harem could not resist his sudden fancy. He had the wife of one of his officers kidnaped while the officer was away on campaign with the whole army. When Bathsheba became pregnant, David wanted to hide his adultery and let the legitimate husband take responsibility for the coming child. He then called Uriah to Jerusalem on the pretext of bringing information. But, whether by fidelity to the rule of temporary continence imposed on combatants or by shrewdness in cleverly invoking an honorable motive, Uriah did not cooperate with the royal maneuver; he did not go to his own house. David then resolved to have him die in the war, and gave orders that he be exposed at the most dangerous point of the battle. A prophet, Nathan, did not let this hidden crime pass without protest. The king repented and was pardoned by Yahweh. Nevertheless, he made Bathsheba his favorite and even designated Solomon, the son she had given him, as his successor (2 Sam. 11:1-24). But this illustrious example of guilty love was to have imitators in its own family. Crime begets crime, and one sinner serves as the providential instrument for the punishment of an earlier sinner.

Weak toward his passions, David was weak, too, toward his children; he avoided reproving them (1 Kings 1:6). Amnon, his heir apparent, was so in love with his half-sister, Tamar, that it made him ill. Unwilling to wait to marry her legally, as would probably have been possible according to ancient customs, he enticed her into a trap and raped her. Having satisfied his desire, he immediately experienced a hatred for the young girl even stronger than his previous love, and he ignominiously threw her out. Absalom, born of the same mother as Tamar, avenged in blood the outrage committed against his sister (2 Sam. 13:1-38). This terrible series of crimes and punishments, the result of a wayward love, is recounted at length in David's family history, and stands as Scripture's most detailed example of the corruption of love by sensual desire.

In Proverbs, the woman takes the initiative in seduction: profiting from her husband's absence, an adulterous wife tries to seduce a naïve young man and succeeds by dint of coaxing words (Prov. 7:6-27).

Samson had been cruelly betrayed by his wife. But in Israel the more common case was that of masculine infidelity leading to divorce, which only the husband could initiate. The prophet Malachi (Mal. 2:13-16) describes the irremediable grief that this provoked. To send away the wife wedded in one's youth is to perform an action hateful to Yahweh, who can no longer look favorably on the victim offered by the author of such a perfidy. God stands as witness between the spouses, whether because He was explicitly invoked by a solemn oath when the marriage was contracted (Prov. 2:17; Ezek. 16:8) or because He knows all the disloyalties of men as an observer whom none can deceive (cf. Gen. 31:50). By mentioning the time of youth, the prophet wishes to recall the love that reigned between the spouses when their union was made (cf. Prov. 5:18; Isa. 54:6; Jer. 2:2); the man is guilty of permitting this love to die.

Solomon, the prestigious king, had been loved by God (2 Sam. 12:24; Neh. 13:26); but he did not respond to this divine attention. His love was for foreign women, married undoubtedly for political reasons, in order to seal an alliance with neighboring sovereigns. And his wives won him over to the veneration of their gods (1 Kings 11:1-8). He succumbed to the great danger of mixed marriages: the abandonment of Yahweh, the God of Israel.

The crass idolatry of Solomon can be succeeded by an idolatry more subtle: that of making the human partner the heart's supreme good. Christ warns His disciples against homage rendered to the creature in place of the Creator: "If a man comes to me without hating his father, mother, wife, children, brothers, sisters, yes and his own life too, he cannot be my disciple" (Luke 14:26). "To hate" is taken in the sense of "to love less," according to the Semitic taste for unqualified contrasts; this can be seen from a parallel passage, one which omits the mention of the wife: "Anyone who prefers father or mother to me is not worthy of me" (Matt. 10:37).

These somber episodes gleaned from the Bible clearly show that the ideal picture traced in the account of woman's creation (Gen. 2:18-25) did not lead to a failure to recognize the debasements to which the malice of sinners had exposed the union of man and woman: racial bonds prevailing over the marriage bond, infidelity, harshness, subjection to sensual passion, abandonment of the true God. If the Old Testament exalted the love between man and woman very highly, it was nonetheless not ignorant of all the deformations that threatened it. It makes us feel the necessity of divine grace so that the exemplary image it has sketched might become a reality.

VII.

HUMAN MARRIAGE: TYPE OF
THE ALLIANCE WITH GOD

The Old Testament often speaks of the human reality of the conjugal union in order to describe its goals, its realizations, and its duties. Yet the Old Testament has contributed in another way to raising the ideal of this union. The prophets compared the alliance between Yahweh and His people to a marriage.[1] A wonderful interchange thus took place between the two realities: the alliance was penetrated by love, instead of being simply a relationship between sovereign and subjects; and the association of man and woman acquired a transcendent model that called marriage to perfect itself.

The prophets did not begin from scratch. The idea of a divine marriage was not unknown to the pagan world of the ancient East. A god could unite with a goddess, with a simple mortal, even with a female animal. Sensuality and generation were the whole meaning of these unions, and constituted the exemplary archetype of the forces of fruitfulness on earth. It was the cycle of life and reproduction that attracted attention in the myths and ritual celebrations. But Israel's prophets transform these notions radically. In their songs, Yahweh weds not an individual woman, but the chosen nation. As was customary among the inspired writers in their use of anthropomorphic language, all imagery too directly sensual or sexual was avoided. But it was impossible to avoid entirely some expressions that might have a more precise sexual meaning alongside a broader sense. Neverthless, phrases like "you will come to know Yahweh" (Hos. 2:22) or "you became mine" (Ezek. 16:8) do not in fact have a properly erotic meaning in these allegories. This reserve is all the more remarkable, since the prophets speak at times of the children which the wedded nation gave Yahweh. Such remarks could have led to describing how the children had been conceived, but this is not the case.

The union of God with His people does not manifest desire but a love full of generosity and tenderness. Yahweh gives, is given, forgives: He does not seek His own advantage, but the good of her whom He loves. Nonetheless He desires to be loved, for He is not a distant Lord, somewhat disdainful in His kindness. The reactions of His jealousy and His anger in the face of Israel's repeated infidelities finally succeed in bringing back to Him the spouse who had turned away to look for adulterous lovers. Love has the last word, a love shared after the tragic vicissitudes of treason, rejection, conversion.

Thus the love of spouses is solemnly consecrated. Marriage is not and should not be simply the institutional framework of the propagation of a race, but the seat of an extremely personal exchange between the partners; a generous tenderness should penetrate marriage. The conclusion was not drawn explicitly by the prophets, as it was to be by St. Paul. But even without giving an explicit lesson such as one finds in the Gospel parables, the model presented by the prophets was able to wield an effective influence. The story of Hosea, the first to develop this conjugal symbolism, seems indeed to be that of a deceived husband demonstrating a persevering and merciful love similar to that of Yahweh for Israel.

In obedience to God's Word, Hosea "married a whore" (Hos. 1:2)—whether he knew or suspected from the outset the fickle character of the spouse he married under a formal divine command or whether more simply, reflecting later, on his misfortunes, he recognized that his marriage had been the result of a providential disposition hidden at first. Children were born and given symbolic names, expressing the legal father's doubt or even his refusal to consider them his own. Finally the unfaithful wife is driven from the home and reduced to slavery; while she is in this humiliation, the prophet is commanded to buy her back and love her again (Hos. 3:1). But a period of penance and seclusion must precede the resumption of the common life.

This tragic story—such as we can piece it together from its disparate elements—was a replica of Yahweh's attitude toward His people. As mediator between God and men, the prophet must experience toward men the very feelings of God, such as the jealousy of which St. Paul will speak to the Corinthian community (2 Cor. 11:2). Hosea himself felt for his own wife that very divine jealousy so often depicted in the Old Testament.[2] Yahweh is a jealous God who will not tolerate sharing with other gods the homages of the nation destined to enter into a nuptial alliance with Him. He punishes His partner when she is unfaithful to Him. But in spite of all the threats, this rejection is never definitive. He wants this spouse to remain His in the end. Abandonment and temporary remoteness are a means of provoking shame and repentance.

In this unique mixture of righteous severity and merciful pardon, where Yahweh always has the initiative, Hosea found the inspiration for his own conduct and gave a singularly new example. Later, the wisdom writers advise as a punishment for adultery only the pitiless dismissal of the unfaithful wife (Prov. 18:22, Greek). But in an era when the law punished adultery by death (Lev. 20:10; Deut. 22:22), Hosea did not show merely an obliging tolerance for his wife's failings, but a loving patience that worked to reconquer the heart of the unworthy spouse. Love was the stronger; but the lesson was so sublime that it was understood only gradually. It will always stand, for wronged partners, as a call to heroism rather than a strict law of Christian marriage. A less difficult solution to the situation created by a guilty partner can be indefinite separation, i.e., separation without prospect of later reunion.

[1]The passages where the prophets developed the matrimonial allegory of Yahweh and Israel are the following, listed in chronological order: Hos. 1-3; Jer. 2-4; 31:21-22; Ezek. 16; 23; Isa. 49:14-23; 50:1; 51:17-52:2; 54:1-14; 57:7-11; 60:1-16; 61:10; 62:1-5. Many of these texts are concerned with depicting and deploring the prostitutions of Israel. Only the earliest text, that of Hosea, calls for particular study here, since it contains an example of human fidelity.

[2]The following texts, among others, express this jealousy, which does not exclude persistent affection and renewal of love: Exod. 20:5-6; 34:14; Deut. 4:24; 6:15; 32:16-21; Isa. 59:17; 63:15; Ezek. 16:38-42; 36:5-7; 39:25; Joel 2:18; Zech. 1:14-15; 8:2.

VIII.

THE NEW TESTAMENT, COMPLETION OF THE OLD

The New Testament does not bring with it any essentially original element by comparison with what we find in the earlier Scriptures. What is new is the manner in which scattered themes, until then more or less foreign to one another, are related to, illuminated, and strengthened by, one another. The recapitulation and concentration of the manifold words of God in a single Word, Christ, and in the religious life of His followers is a universal matter.

Jesus recalled first of all that marriage should be regulated not only by properly juridic prescriptions, but above all by the great directives found in the creation accounts of Genesis (Matt. 19:3-9, quoting Gen. 1:27 and 2:24). The specific object to which Jesus applied this principle is divorce, which Moses tolerated because of men's hardness of heart, even though it was contrary to the Creator's intention. The two spouses are from then on but one body, that is, one unity made by God himself, which man is guilty of wanting to divide. In His answer to the Pharisees the Master does not foresee the sterility of a marriage as permitting it to be dissolved. He did not quote Genesis 1:28, which expressed God's

blessing of fruitfulness and which followed immediately upon the verse He had just recalled. This is not
meant, of course, to imply that fruitfulness is an outdated value. He simply sees that marriage is not
instituted exclusively in view of procreation. It
draws value also from the very close companionship
it sets up between the spouses.

The apostles were often concerned to give the
faithful directives about their family life. We can
begin by considering three rather similar texts, which
in our day are liable to awaken some astonishment,
to say nothing of scandal: 1 Peter 3:1-7; Colossians
3:18-19; Ephesians 5:22-23.

St. Peter does not even use the word "love." He
remains within Jewish thought patterns which insisted
on the pre-eminence of the husband and the dependence of the wife, and he quotes the example of Sarah
giving Abraham the name "Lord" (Gen. 18:12). By
her good conduct a submissive wife can be more
effective in the conversion of an unbelieving husband
than can the Church's preaching. Nonetheless men
must not act like tyrants. In their married life, they
must not only take into account the lesser physical
strength of their companions, but also treat them
with honor and recognize their fundamental equality
in the possession of divine grace (1 Pet. 1-7). Likewise slaves ought to respect their masters, recalling
the example of Christ, who was unjustly mistreated
(1 Pet. 2:18, 25; cf. Titus 2:9-10).

When St. Paul sketches, in the Epistle to the

Colossians (3:18-4:1), the mutual duties of wife and husband, of children and of parents, of slaves and of masters, he keeps the same conservative perspective. He begins with the partner on whom devolves the duty of dependence, so that he might later urge the other partner not to abuse his superiority. He enjoins husbands to love their wives and not to show themselves harsh toward them. We find the same pattern in the Epistle to the Ephesians (5:22-6:9)—an invitation, on the one hand, to submission and, on the other, to moderation in the exercise of authority. But the emphasis is modified by a long addition on conjugal love, to which we will return.

It is worthwhile to anticipate the uneasiness sometimes caused today by these prescriptions; they seem so unconcerned about questioning an established social order and wondering if it respects providential intentions. We are tempted to say that the apostles are satisfied to pour just a few drops of the new wine of the Gospels into the old wineskins of Judaism, undoubtedly to avoid their bursting (cf. Matt. 9:17). But before we feel scandalized by their attitude, we must ponder the conduct of Christ himself.

When the Pharisees try to trap Jesus by asking if it is permissible to pay taxes to Caesar, He avoids the theoretical question of the legitimacy of the Roman occupation (Matt. 22:15-22). If the emperor were only an unjust invader, he would not deserve obedience or, therefore, tribute. From this point of view, one could easily conclude to the duty of violent insurrection. When questioned, the Master limits himself to remarking that the common currency is that of Caesar. Thus it matters little for this question whether the occupation is just or not; the occupier's administration in fact performs useful services, which justify a certain degree of submission on the part of the Jews. Let them think of fulfilling their duties toward God before wondering whether the Roman control is legitimate suzerainty or unjust tyranny. The point of the parable of the splinter and the plank is that self-correction must precede the desire to correct others (Matt. 7:3-5).

The apostles sketch a similar pattern of behavior for the first Christian generation in the face of social inequalities which they do not necessarily approve (of which they even disapprove, as their language indicates), but which they could not suppress on the spot without provoking greater disorders. They urge the Christians to see in the actual situation the good it has kept, without closing their eyes to abuses of slavery or of paternal or marital authority.[1]

We can now understand better the rich developments in the text of Ephesians 5:22-33, which constitutes a higher synthesis of views scattered through the Old Testament. If wives are exhorted from the outset to submit to their husbands, it is as an application of a more general rule which prescribes that the faithful should give way to one another in obedience to Christ (Eph. 5:21). This is, then, reciprocity, not unilateral predominance. Husbands must love their wives as Christ loved the Church, with a generous love that does not hesitate before sacrifice. Christ therefore filled the spouse's role that the prophets had attributed to Yahweh; both showed the same loving care for the spouse, who is first purified by a bath, then adorned (Eph. 5:26-27; Ezek. 16:8-14). But the apostle soon remembers Genesis 2:24. Woman was taken from the body of man and ought to return to him. Thus the husband should love his wife, since she is his own body; he should look after her and feed her, as he would do for his own body (Eph. 5:28-29). The biblical citation "a man must leave his father and mother and be joined to his wife, and the two will become one body" helps us to understand what Paul is trying to say. Physical union is a normal manifestation of the love that ought to unite the spouses; it is of course not the only manifestation, but conjugal society requires this sign and this basis. Thanks to the gradual purifications of the Old Testament, Paul can bring together the thought of Christ and the notion of sexual union more freely than the prophets had dared to do in speaking of Yahweh and Israel. He is no longer faced with the spectacle of the pagan fertility cults that often contaminated the Chosen People. He rediscovered in the Eden account of Genesis 2 the initial purity of the couple as God had created it. There is nothing sinful in conjugal life itself. Love must penetrate its bodily elements just as it eliminates all trace of the wife's servile dependence.

The doctrine of the Church, body of Christ, a doctrine proper to Paul, is a new and fuller application of the thought found in the Old Testament. Just

as a social group forms an organism (body and flesh)
whose members recognize one another as such; just
as, in Genesis 2:23, the couple is the closest of
societies, so for Paul the Church forms the most
perfect, most vast, and most closely bound society
with Christ who is her head. This idea dominated
Pauline sexual morality.

Just as husband and wife are destined to become
a single body, so, in Paul's view, all the disciples of
Christ, in union with their risen Lord, ought to form
one great body whose parts are vitally related to
one another. The small associations into which the
members of Christ's body enter must not then lead
them in a direction contrary to that which animates
this great whole. The body of every individual is
destined for the Lord, not for debauchery. Union
with a prostitute makes a man one body with her;
this is a perverse degradation of the marital union.
Instead of stable affection, capable of being governed
by charity, sensuality and selfishness are the motives
for the lustful encounter. This is incompatible with
union with Christ. A man cannot take parts of Christ's
body and join them to the body of a prostitute
(1 Cor. 6:12-20).

On the other hand, the small conjugal society is
homogeneous with the larger society which is the
body of Christ. Speaking absolutely, celibacy is
undoubtedly preferable, to the degree that it permits
undivided attachment to the Lord. But not all have
been given that gift. Marriage, too, is a gift from
God (1 Cor. 7:7-8; 7:32-35). In many concrete cases

it is the better course, for sexual misconduct is a very real danger. "It is better to be married than to be tortured" (1 Cor. 7:9).

In this text marriage appears as a remedy for concupiscence and a precaution against sin. But this must be put back into the general framework of Paul's thought, which is not that of a scrupulous legalism. The apostle places charity above everything (1 Cor. 13:13); by love of neighbor a man fulfills all the commandments (Rom. 13:8-9). Through Christian marriage, charity governs (or can govern) the sexual impulse; it is oriented in a healthy direction instead of away from it. The married Christian will find it easier "to keep away from fornication and to know how to use the body that belongs to him in a way that is holy and honorable, not giving way to selfish lust like the pagans who do not know God."[2] The encounter with the true God has transformed the encounter with the other in marriage; physical desire is no longer primary.

When Paul proposes marriage as an escape from debauchery, he formulates his thought in a negative form, and thus clearly shows that he does not yet think very highly of the moral level of the Corinthians to whom he is writing. This is also why he speaks of sexual relations between the spouses in terms of a debt to be rendered instead of in terms of love. But the profound meaning of these verses (1 Cor. 7:3-4) is in harmony with that of Ephesians 5:28, which urges husbands to love their wives because they are their husbands' own bodies.

It is remarkable that Paul mentions only the mutual debt of the spouses when he gives his opinions on the use of marriage. His perspective is that of Genesis 2:23. He does not draw the justification of sexual union directly from fruitfulness; but he does not forget that the couples he is addressing ordinarily have children (1 Cor. 7:14). In the Pastoral Epistles, the work of his old age, the apostle will no longer propose celibacy as an alternative; he will insist almost exclusively on the most common vocation of young women: to get married, to have children, to govern their homes (1 Tim. 5:14), and to love their husbands and their children (Titus 2:4). The wife will be saved by childbearing (1 Tim. 2:15), according to the common understanding of this text, or perhaps simply through childbearing, without finding in it either an obstacle to, or a specific means of, salvation. It is perseverence in faith, love, and holiness that assures salvation (1 Tim. 2:15). In opposition to those who forbid marriage (1 Tim. 4:3), Paul affirms the goodness of that state and of procreation, which it generally involves.[3]

The action of parents is not limited to bringing their children into the world. In line with the whole biblical tradition, Paul reminds parents of their educative task. In Ephesians 5:22-6:4 and Colossians 3:18-21, he views family duties in their double polarity: mutual duties of the spouses and mutual duties of parents and children. In this he breaks with the Old Testament, which always separated the two perspectives. It is necessary to avoid an excessive severity, which would exasperate the children and risk driving them to resentment or frustration (Eph. 6:4; Col. 3:21). On the contrary, paternal lessons must appear like a discipline coming from the Lord himself (Eph. 6:4). Knowing how to direct his children firmly is one of the criteria that augur well for a presbyter or a bishop (1 Tim. 3:4; Titus 1:6) or for a widow (1 Tim. 5:10). This task does not stop with the early years; young women still need the prudent advice of their mothers (Titus 2:4). This education transmits more than simply a worldly formation: Timothy knows by experience that he owes his faith to his mother and his grandmother (2 Tim. 1:5).

Paul turns his attention at times to the normal fruitfulness of the couple, at times to the unity they form. He never implies that generation is the unique end of the sexual function. Furthermore, such an oversimplification would harmonize poorly with his deep feeling for the complexity of the organism. Speaking about the teaching on the body of Christ, he mentions not only the multiplicity of parts and the diversity of their functions, but also the somewhat ambiguous variety of aspects that the same organ can have. The improper parts are treated with more modesty. God himself "has arranged the body so that more dignity is given to the parts which are without it, and so that there may not be disagreements inside the body" (1 Cor. 12:22-25). In fact it is the sexual organ which receives circumcision, the sign of the alliance (Gen. 17:11); and it is this organ which, in the patriarchal epoch, was touched in the sacred gesture of the oath (Gen. 24:2; 47:29). The complexity of the body and the close bonds existing between contrary qualities prevent any simplification to a single viewpoint. Paul sees fruitfulness in the life of the couple as well as the relationships uniting the spouses, relationships which must develop into an ever deeper love. He did not try to set up a hierarchy, and to hope to find such a hierarchy would be to risk understanding the flexibility of his thought.

The biblical testimony, considered in its totality, has manifested a rich variety. Different values have been discovered in the course of the centuries, and they have come to expression in the holy books. It is in the Epistles of St. Paul that the different themes developed before him were most thoroughly reorganized; but this is not to say that he has deprived the earlier writings of all value. On the contrary, his Epistles can only be well understood by using this anticipated commentary.

To sum up the teaching of Scripture in a few words: Sexuality and its legitimate use in marriage assume a double aspect: fruitfulness, which calls new lives into existence, and the love which the spouses bear for one another. These two aspects interpenetrate inextricably. Both constitute an imitation of God; neither is to be placed above the other. Man must respect a living reality that surpasses the over-simplifying limits of his mind. He must respect a divine work where every part has its value, instead of tending to valorize one element unduly by attributing to it a pre-eminent place. God alone deserves absolute homage. As for creatures, "You must not say, 'This is worse than that,' for everything will prove its value in its time" (Sirach 39:34).

[1]There is no reason to repeat here the passages where St. Paul speaks of the image of God in man; they have been grouped above (pp. 12-14) around the basic text of Gen. 1:27. Their result is the proclamation of the essential equality of the sexes.

[2]1 Thess. 4:4-5. This passage probably concerns the husband's own body, although one might understand it as referring to the wife's body, which belongs to the husband (cf. 1 Cor. 7:4). This hardly changes the basic idea. Paul may have been inspired here by Tobit 8:5 according to the text of the Vulgate, if this reflects an old textual tradition. Tobias tells his wife that they cannot unite themselves like the pagans who do not know God and that they must first give themselves to prayer.

[3]In a milieu where the sufferings of childbearing were attributed to a divine judgment (Gen. 3:16), where the woman was ritually unclean for long weeks after the birth of her child (Lev. 12), the conclusion could be easily drawn that it was good not to bear children. One of Jesus' listeners, Salome, formulates such a conclusion in the apocryphal Gospel according to the Egyptians. Paul reacts against this erroneous depreciation of fruitfulness. Childbearing is a normal thing; a woman can bear children without danger to her salvation.

CONCLUSION:

TOWARD A SYNTHESIS

After seeking out what the biblical books have to say on the double theme of love and fruitfulness, it would be well to take a final look at what we have found, with a view toward synthesis and in order to highlight the more lasting values. In this domain as in others, the Word of God is essentially dynamic and pedagogical. The inspired authors in no way present a systematic notion of marriage, entirely complete from the very beginning. With great realism, they base themselves on ideas and practices customary in their milieu, and are content to perfect these ideas and practices in one particular aspect. Thus in the New Testament, theoretically outdated views, such as the constitutional dependence of women, retain a certain place, at least at first. We must then bring out more clearly the highest values that Scripture expresses on the subject we are considering. These are ordinarily found in the New Testament, but they are sometimes in the Old Testament as well. For the gospel message, making its own the whole law and the prophets by a general confirmation (Matt. 5:17-19), did not always repeat in so many words the entire content of the manifold revelation which God had addressed to Israel's ancestors through the centuries preceding Christ's coming.

THE NEW TESTAMENT, COMPLETION OF THE OLD 71

Thus Scripture will appear as meeting the contemporary preoccupations of Christian couples about subjects such as the freedom of their commitment, the equality of their society, the growth of their love, and the place fruitfulness has in it.

1. Freedom of commitment should be an essential charactertistic in the Christian concept of marriage, in contrast to what one finds presupposed in the Old Testament and to the constraint that sometimes exists even in a Christian milieu. This is not simply a question of the result of contemporary social facts. For instance, since marriage is contracted today at a less precocious age than in ancient Israel, the greater maturity of engaged persons would lead to increased consideration of their desires. Or again, since the work activity of young people is now independent of the familial framework, they would not be obliged to take into account familial imperatives in the choice of a life companion. But what is above all essential to the New Alliance is to respect the individual responsibility of each of the faithful. A member of this community of the New Alliance is not simply bound by ties of familial or social solidarity. He is also in a direct relation with the God who writes the law in his heart. In a very important oracle, which was taken up again in the Epistle to the Hebrews (Jer. 31:29-34; Heb. 8:8-12), the prophet Jeremiah defined the fundamental charter of the new relationships that must be set up: "Deep within them I will plant my Law, writing it on their hearts. . . . There will be no further need for neighbor to try to teach neighbor,

or brother to say to brother, 'Learn to know Yahweh!' No, they will all know me, the least no less than the greatest." This text does not speak explicitly of marriage. But in such a religious economy, a commitment that decides the whole course of later life should proceed from personal will and not from the initiative of the head of the family.[1]

We find here again the same thing that was suggested by the reflection which drew the moral from the creation of woman: "This is why a man leaves his father and mother and joins himself to his wife" (Gen. 2:24). We can appreciate the validity of the fiancée's protests in the Song of Songs against the excessive interference of her brothers, who are deciding her marriage in advance (see above, pp. 42-43). In this perspective, some of the maxims of the wisdom writings take on a new, fuller meaning. Whereas it was commonly held that a father gave his daughter in marriage or chose a wife for his son, the wisdom writers held that a virtuous wife comes from Yahweh himself (Prov. 18:22; 19-14; Sirach 26:3).

Disorders which had weakened traditional social ties in Israel had probably favored a more lively appreciation of personal values. Thus the establishment of the monarchy under Saul and David weakened the cohesion of the patriarchal clans and made possible greater individual freedom in the nation. The redaction of the Yahweh traditions, among which is the account of woman's creation (Gen. 2), is usually dated from this time. The deportation to Babylon destroyed the national monarchy and separated families; it was then that Jeremiah proclaimed his message of the New Alliance. External circumstances had their part in provoking a given inspired writer to commit one or another idea to writing. But the inspiration of Scripture assures us that these ideas were not just the contingent reaction of a human mind, but also the Word of God.

2. The equality of the partners is not simply a demand of the modern mind; it is a requirement of love. The Song of Songs already gives it concrete expression. It is a remote consequence of faith in an infinitely transcendent God, to whose eyes all differences between creatures are nothing. The apostolic Epistles take the actual situation of the day into account and speak of the wife's submission; but at the same time they give such an expression the necessary corrective.

The wife will not be subject to her husband as a slave; each depends on the other. There is no point in expecting Scripture to furnish a rule that would settle all difficulties in advance. Scripture only gives general exhortations. Love is never selfish (1 Cor. 13:5). Serve one another in works of love (Gal. 5:13). Bear with one another charitably (Eph. 4:2). Give way to one another in obedience to Christ (Eph. 5:21).

In normal daily life the wife will have an initiative and a responsibility that her husband will not think to contest. He will rely on her for the care of the home. This is shown by the poem on the perfect wife (Prov. 31:10-31), which nevertheless was composed in a predominantly masculine milieu. Paul, in turn, presumes that young married women will have their homes to look after (1 Tim. 5:14).

The Bible ordinarily speaks of the woman's work as being in the home; this is only to be expected in the setting in which the Bible was redacted, an economy where agriculture itself was most often familial. In another economic system, the partners' equality could be realized by the wife's working outside the home. There is already such a case in Scripture in the example of Tobit and Anna (Tobit 2:11-12). This clearly shows that we must not take as absolute, rigid rules those biblical directives which are bound up with determined social situations and which can vary with them.

In a technical society growing more and more complex, it can happen that man, engrossed by his profession, may be led to greater and greater specialization. This could involve the danger of narrowing the properly human outlook on life. The wife, even if she works outside the home, will be less clearly specialized; she must be more completely concerned with all the needs and aspects of life. Since she will not always have a technical or intellectual competence equal to that of her husband, she will be able to remain more easily open to everything and to know better how to create a favorable atmosphere for her home and her children. Here again we find an equality which is not interchangeable.

3. The growth and maturation of love is a problem

not explicitly considered by the New Testament. But the conclusion of the Song of Songs (8:6-7) develops this point:

> Set me like a seal on your heart, . . .
> For love is strong as Death, . . .
> The flash of it is a flash of fire, . . .
> Love no flood can quench.

This impassioned invitation does not simply wish to avert infidelity; it calls to an ever more active life of love. Fire is insatiable (Prov. 30:16); and, following its example, love must strive for constant growth. It will thus be able to triumph over adversity, symbolized by the flood. The burning drive, the yearning for always deeper union that animates the biblical poem ought to be seen as well in the love to which St. Paul exhorts Christian husbands (Eph. 5:25-33). Even if it is a love which comes after marriage, it should not be just a kindness that excludes severity and authoritarianism toward feminine weakness. It must always look for new food, like the fire; that is, it must always strive to include all the domains of the spouses' lives.

Conjugal love should not be limited to sensual exaltation, nor to concern for common temporal interests. It must extend to the common search for eternal salvation. Even in a marriage where only one of the partners is Christian, he ought to hope for the conversion of the non-Christian and, as far as possible, prepare the way for it. When he speaks of such a case (1 Cor. 7:12-16), St. Paul recognizes that this hope will not always be fulfilled. But this does not stop him from recalling the extent to which marriage should make real the unity of life. St. Peter in turn teaches that a pious wife's silent example can have a more effective influence on an unbelieving husband than preaching (1 Pet. 3:1-2). There is all the more reason for mutual love to include the spiritual interests of spouses already united in the same faith. Each can imitate Christ, who sacrificed himself for the salvation of the Church (Eph. 5:26). Each can make up for the sake of his partner what still has to be undergone by Christ, as Paul did for the Church, whose servant he had become (Col. 1:24).

The love of spouses ought to be in accord with the love of God, and not contrary to it. The two loves of God and of neighbor are inseparable in the practice of the Christian life. They grow together; they do not coexist by means of reciprocal limitations and concessions. The same holds true for the life of marriage, but particular difficulties enter here. If conjugal love finds its deepest source in the love of God, it will occasionally give up some of its most human manifestations to promote the growth of divine love. Paul recommends that the couples of Corinth abstain from conjugal relations temporarily, in order to give themselves to prayer with more fervor (1 Cor. 7:5-6). He would almost wish that the love of spouses could divest itself of any sexual dimension and be transformed into a pure spiritual friendship. But he knows that this is not possible, because not all have received this gift (1 Cor. 7:7).

At the very least, conjugal love must not be an

idolatry of the partner; it must be subordinated to the love of God. This is difficult, for both of these loves have an exclusive character. The married Christian therefore feels divided and drawn in opposite directions (1 Cor. 7:33). But he can avert the threat of a conflict. "Those who have wives should live as though they had none" (1 Cor. 7:29). This does not refer to an effective rupture of conjugal life or to emotional indifference, but to living like those who, by a sovereign attachment to God, can deal with the world without becoming engrossed in it (1 Cor. 7:31). Conjugal love will then be able to grow as it must in a vivifying tension with the love of God.

4. Fruitfulness is a fact which imposes itself on the majority of couples and which has to be integrated into the growth of their love. If there is no question of fruitfulness in the love poem of the Song of Songs (except by implication), it is because the lovers are young, for whom the prospect of future offspring is relatively remote, and because the whole cultural milieu kept them quite aware of this prospect. The wisdom writings and the apostolic Epistles consider these two characteristics of conjugal life, i.e., love and fruitfulness; but they say little about their relationship. Such statements are, however, quite possible in a Christian view.

The child must be a part of the mutual love of his parents. He is its assurance—not only as the fruit, and thus the reminder, of past union, but as the lasting invitation to the common task of education. In him the love of the spouses is preserved from the element of idolatry that can enter into an exclusive emotion closed in on itself: the partner is no longer the be-all and end-all; each opens to a third, their child.

In him each parent gives a gift that fulfills the other's desire to be a father or a mother. But this is not a danger for their mutual love, as if the child whom they gave to one another threatened to draw to himself the spouses' mutual love; nor does he threaten to become the unique reason for the continuance of an association that would no longer need the allurement of love.

Thanks to the child, conjugal love is enriched with a previously unknown dimension, or at least a dimension desired but not in fact possessed. Instead of centering on its own happiness and risking being taken for granted, the parents' mutual love is engaged in an activity where each will have to give for a long time before thinking of receiving in return. The Christian, who ought to find more happiness in giving than in receiving,[2] can experience such a joy in the long task of education. The two spouses share this happiness by their fruitfulness, rather than by closing themselves in on their mutual union. By joining in the patient effort of a common action whereby they educate their children, they open a new dimension to their own love and permit that love to mature.

Such are the data which the Word of God can offer us about these two values of love and fruitfulness, values that give meaning to the common life of a couple. Our understanding of these texts is not independent of the effort exerted by the Christian people through the centuries to practice their demands. When Christian preaching entered the Greco-Roman pagan milieu, where marriage was above all else an institution intended to perpetuate a family and, officially at least, separate from love, it slowly reformed the mentality and the morals. To the degree that it did so, Scripture better revealed its hidden treasures. In this way, for example, the Song of Songs is better understood in our days as a love song, and thus as containing a very important lesson on sexuality and marital union. It is no longer commonly held that an apparently worldly song must necessarily have an allegorical religious intent in order to be included in the holy books. Theologians are beginning to use it in their approach to marriage, just as they are coming to understand better what the Epistle to the Ephesians has to say about conjugal love.

New situations will arise in the future; facts neglected till now will manifest themselves to a more attentive study of present and of past. Such things can lead us to hear the Word of God with new ears; for it is inexhaustible, and we can never boast that we have taken its full measure. Here as elsewhere St. Augustine's invitation holds good: "Let us therefore seek as having [still] to discover, and discover as having [still] to seek."[3]

[1]This fundamental freedom of choice naturally does not deny that it is ordinarily opportune to have recourse to parental

experience before making a definitive decision.

[2]The statement of Christ, "There is more happiness in giving than in receiving," is reported by St. Paul in a speech (Acts 20:35), but it is not found in the Gospels. It can be compared to Luke 14:14.

[3]Augustine, **De Trinitate**, IX, 1; PL 42, 961.

SELECTED BIBLIOGRAPHY

Barth, Karl, **Kirchliche Dogmatik,** III (1945).

Cole, W. G., **Sex and Love in the Bible** (London: Hodder and Stoughton, 1960). Treats of divine love and human love of neighbor as well as of the love between man and woman; discusses sexual failings.

Daniel-Rops, Henri, **De l'amour humain dans la Bible** (Strasbourg-Paris: F. X. Le Roux, 1950); 96 pages and many illustrations.

Du Buit, M., **La famille et la Bible,** Cahiers "Evangile," No. 63 (July, 1966).

Grelot, P., **Le couple humain dans la Bible** (Lectio divina, No. 31); (Paris: Ed. du Cerf, 1962); previously appeared in **Supplement de la Vie Spirituelle** (1961), pp. 135-198. The author limited himself to the couple, apart from the question of fruitfulness.

Kerns, J. E., **The Theology of Marriage.** The Historical Development of Christian Attitudes toward Sex and Sanctity in Marriage (New York, Sheed & Ward, 1964). An anthology of material on marriage and sexuality, from the first to the twentieth centuries. Each section includes a summary of, and commentary on, biblical passages.

Murphy, R. E., **Seven Books of Wisdom** (Milwaukee: Bruce Publishing Company, 1960); pp. 67-86: The Song of Love.

Orrieux, J., **Vocation de la femme: recherche biblique,** pp. 139-159, in **La femme, nature et vocation** (Recherches et debats du C.C.I.F., no. 45, December, 1963).

Schillebeeckx, E., **Het Huwelijk. Aardse Werkelijkheid en Heilsmysterie** (1964). Two chapters discuss marriage in the Old and the New Testaments.